FREE SEX CHOCOLATE

Poems & Songs
JULIAN GOUGH

salmonpoetry

Published in 2010 by
Salmon Poetry
Cliffs of Moher, County Clare, Ireland
Website: www.salmonpoetry.com
Email: info@salmonpoetry.com

ISBN 978-1-907056-36-9

Cover artwork: *rolled up magazines* © *Retroman – Fotolia.com*
Cover design & typesetting: *Siobhán Hutson*
Printed in England by imprint*digital*.net

Salmon Poetry receives financial assistance from The Arts Council

To Sophie

Acknowledgements

Poetry, as an affliction, comes and goes, like malaria. I don't know why most of these poems arrived, and when they did arrive, I usually didn't know what to do with them, so this won't be a long list of acknowledgements. Mostly, I've just put them up quietly on my website, to be read by puzzled drunks who've mistyped "porn" into Google. But a couple of them have managed to pop up elsewhere, so...

I'd like to thank Stephen Lydon, who commissioned me to write poems on the flyers for his wonderful clubnight, *Psychedelia*, in The Castle, Galway.

Thanks to Richard Rose (and his brother Phil), for wanting "The Book of Longing has disturbed my sleep" for R*E*P*E*A*T, the excellent punk fanzine.

And thanks to Billy Mills, for letting me try out some of these pieces in "Poster Poems", the vigorous and democratic weekly forum he hosts so well on the Guardian's Books' Blog.

The songs, unlike the poems, were written to be heard, some of them back when I was still a teenager. Many were written, with Neil Farrell and Declan Collins (who wrote all the music for Toasted Heretic), in Neil's parents' livingroom. Some were written, and many were rewritten or improved, with the whole band in the room: Declan, Neil, Aengus McMahon, Breffni O'Rourke, and later Barry Wallace. I'd like to thank them all for those extraordinary years. If there is any music in these words, they put it there. And I'd like to thank Neil's parents, Una and Richard Farrell, for putting up with us, as I learned to be a writer, and we learned to be a band.

Unusually humble thanks to Jessie Lendennie at Salmon for saying "Julian, this is a book."

And finally, very special thanks to Siobhán Hutson for her sensitive and creative work on the layout, proofing, and, particularly, the cover design.

Contents

Part 1 – POEMS

Part 2 – SONGS

Songs for Swinging Celibates (Toasted Heretic, 1988):

Charm & Arrogance (Toasted Heretic, 1989):

The Smug EP (Toasted Heretic, 1990):

Another Day, Another Riot (Toasted Heretic, 1992):

Mindless Optimism (Toasted Heretic, 1994):

B-sides, unreleased tracks, and post-Heretic lyrics:

Part 1: POEMS

The Book of Longing has disturbed my sleep

I

Poems are so hard to read
Who has the time?
I started one in nineteen sixty six
And I still haven't got to the rhyme

II

My daughter says
"I'm cleaning the self"
As she wipes her face with the floor sponge.
She's two in January.

III

I wrote a poem
On my daughter's scribble
And ruined the only piece of art in the house.

IV

I write these tiny poems
At five in the morning
Then pause
And read them over
With a feeling that is neither pleasure nor displeasure
Like a rabbit eating its own droppings.

V

And now we have the internet
And my bad poem can be read in a billion homes.
Now if that isn't progress what is?

VI

Eventually the dawn will screw me up.
But for now I sit on the floor of this flat in Berlin
My back hardly hurts
My pen works
I write a short poem and stop
Pause
Write a short poem, and stop.
The motor of the refrigerator cuts in, and runs for a while,
and stops.

Nothing happens for a while.

The motor kicks in again.

This is good.

VII

Poems are so hard to write
Who has the time?
I started this one in nineteen sixty six.

VIII

I should have written more when I was young
I should have fucked more women.
The only hours I didn't waste.
They add up to so few days.

As I sit here writing this
I hear my women breathing in the other rooms.

IX

You get up at five in the morning
And write poems about poetry for an hour and a half.
You are forty and you have no money and your trousers have
split and nobody reads poetry.
But your wife is beautiful
And your daughter is beautiful
And you're wearing a great shirt.
In a few hours you will all have coffee together.
You make a note at the top of a new page
"Write to Leonard Cohen and thank him before he dies."

X

Of course it would have been nice
To sum it all up in a few lines
And enlighten the world before going back to bed.
But that is what the sun is for
And it does it once a day for free
And it's hard to compete with that.
In fact, here it comes now
Rising over Rückerstrasse
Putting me out of business again.

(December 2006, Rückerstrasse, Berlin)

Doughnuts

Fuck the Greeks and fuck the Romans
We were Homer and Lisa, eating doughnuts
In Weinbergsweg Park
Where the drug dealers go nuts.

Karl kicks his Alsatian
While his radio station
In that gap between Whitney and Britney
Broadcasts the bomb blasts
To the total indifference
Of his mate, playing ping pong
With one arm in a cast

Sophie, who's three, says
"I'm Lisa. I'm eight.
Look how Lisa can write."
Her odyssey in black yellow
Blue green another blue
Purple, and white

Derek Purple was asleep
On the back seat
Of his friend's car
On New Year's Day, near dawn. Nice.

The car went into a skid
Somewhere between Galway and a party
Or a party and Galway
Or a party and another party
I never got the details of the story.

His friend turned back.
Too much black ice.

Homer finished his doughnut, said "Schmecht."
Lisa finished hers, said "Lecker, lecker!"
Homer got the check.

Safely home, he tried to wake
Derek. It took a while to make
The leap, off the map,
And realise that noise
As the spinning car had slammed
To a halt, had been the snap
Of Derek's neck.

Fuck the Greeks and fuck the Romans
With their tragedies and omens
Who needs them when we've got doughnuts
In Weinbergsweg park
Where the drug dealers go nuts.

Dead Teenagers

(for Jon Savage)

Dead teenagers writhe
Between her legs, slide
Across her thighs, drop
Off the side, as she
Paces the tight stage
In front of the projector.

The publisher has introduced the book.
Jon Savage stands.
The evening has begun, look:

The invention of the stars
In 1913. Divine
And human at the same time,
A production line of Christs.

Dwarves, lost in the forest of knees,
Look up the skirts of screaming girls
Who sway in their own breeze
Rioting at
The premiere of
The Wizard of Oz.

The Columbia Day riot in 1943:
Times Square jammed tight
As twenty five thousand young women
Go mad after
Frank Sinatra

That rat pack, not quite
Translating black into white,
While on another planet, fifty streets away

18

(Fifth Avenue!)
Two young! black! gay! women
(Women!)
Touch fingertips for the first time
Breathe in. Freeze.
Hold hands. Commit
A crime.

Back in Berlin
They have forgotten
To click the button
Resizing each photo to fit the screen.
Rudolph Valentino, a member of
The Hitler Youth, a Bright Young Thing,
Two men in ripped zoot suits,
Boy scouts and the unemployed
Drift past, footloose, beheaded.

Hitler inspects his teenage troops.
Women grunt approval of their brutes.

The Northern Rock has dropped
The other rocks are dropping
Where will we all go
If we can't go shopping?

Back, into our trances,
At the animal dances?

Starring James Bond

I have read the fiction
Of Thomas Disch
And Santa Claus
All characters fictitious
Duplicitous, sly.

I hear that Santa Claus
Facing eviction
Shot himself, in the kitchen
On the Fourth of July.

A month before David
Foster
Wallace
Hung himself
(Had he read "Big Blonde"?)

Two months before
Quantum of Solace
Arrived in the cinemas
Starring James Bond.

DNA

I

As a lad,
A bit of a tearaway,
Dan,
Kicked in the nads,
Wipes a tear away

Friends
When the poems appear
Like bruises
Are surprised to hear
Some of the words he chooses

A fruitful childhood's
Ripest moments
Cherry picked
In plummy tones.
The apple of truth
Falls to the ground.
Lies.

Yet
You can't tear your ear away

II

Dan and Amanda's son will be
Fine they say.
Lies.

Dan sits in the dark till it gets bright.

At seven in the morning, the sun rises.

At seven in the mourning, the son rises.

And Dan
Starts to write
His first word of the night.

The letters
Recombine
Like DNA.

Commit

1. Revolting

        Child going through action
    The lock cracks!
Her codes, codings and locks are cracked!
Every sight a revolt
Once around the post office palace, in a historical postal coach.

2. Casting

You grow up
You cast Berlin

Show you're able
Show your Being
Show your muscle
And leave
They, today, discover themselves!
With the casting director and an actress, Greta.

Amen.

3. Misunderstanding

Misunderstandings in the large city
The women say they don't mind
Though again and again
They find the men in an
Open air cinema of the unmistakable kind
In a summer beer garden, in the inner court,
Until one o'clock, in the plenary assembly hall
      Their excuses –
          Szeni representations
            Prussian reforms.

Actors in historical costumes
Put talc down their cleavage
Then yours.

After the avalanche of love,
Under the bodies of skiers,
Snow covered
Hard mountains
Are found. Among other things.

Secateurs.
Non sequiturs.
Cock rings.

Historical figures of 1808
Place themselves, authentically, above visitors like you
Insert themselves, and wait.

4. Meeting

Meeting place: the bar in the
Information Container.
You saw, on the screens
In his eyes
Scenes from the life, should the dead ones
Accompany you to the other world
Like a toilet.
Welcome, drunkenness
Welcome, hunt scenes, car running and fist fights

Under it
Seven fully constant graves, from the 5th century before
Christ, Axel Springer and the German unit.

5. Cornering

Watch her
Corner the Japanese guards
Just like copies of her extensive personal collection
    of short-lived objects.
She makes them guard her extensive personal collection
    of short-lived objects.
One thousand nine hundred and eighty nine
Short-lived objects.

Half-lives unknown

6. Exhibiting

From hoses and balls we build fairy tale nature.
In the pool, the free area, we test can they swim.

An exhibition of the hidden museum
Must be held in the visible museum

The collection: Berlin the
Radical
Divided
Border power comedy.

After the action, reaction.
Collapse and retraction of the hardon.
You sing! Play! Dance!
Pretend it never happened.
Bees practice
Seduction in the garden

7. *Committing*

They say commitment is impossible
In this age of blood and irony
In this place of all places.

OK, yes,
The committer finds it hard
To meet the committee.

But, don't forget,
With the wind to the west,
They swarmed also by night
Down Lime Tree Road
For a short time before that
Famous collapse
In price
For art
Electricity
Natural gas, and John Hurt.

And yet, still, at night, in
This city, or despite it,
Unusual faces – in their ways – commit.

Pay Me What You Owe Me

I muse
On how the national attitudes
To money and to art
Are expressed at the point where
They pay you for the reading

In Geneva, the green
Hundred euro notes
Crisp from the bank machine

In Prague, the very thought
Of mentioning a fee despicable

In the city of London
The P.R., the invoice
The choice of cheque or
Electronic transfer
The request for VAT number, if applicable.
The answer.

(In Berlin
I turned up
A month late
By mistake
Thus negating
The need
For a fee)

In Zagreb, the possibility
That a European funding body
Might pay you something, soon.

In Charlie Byrne's
In Galway, my doubloon
A hardback of Horse Latitudes
By Paul Muldoon.

These Are A Few of the Things That I Hate

Impetus.
That's another of the fuckers.
Along with limned
And luminous
And the world made new after fecking rain
And the single word of Irish, placed with sugar tongs
In among the undistinguished English,
With its grant-supported fada at a jaunty golden angle
Like a single fresh-thatched roof on an industrial estate.

Drivetime in Fog

They are flying on instruments
Starting before dawn
When the alarm goes off.
They walk in their sleep
To the kitchen
And eat because it is eating time
And drive because it is drivetime
At eighty because it's the limit
For the zone.

Machinery brings them
To a floor with a number
Corresponding to
Height from the ground

The ground itself
The height
The speed
The drive
The food
The dawn
Are all invisible
Because of the fog

Much later
The clock on the computer
Tells them to stop working.
As they are leaving
The lift gets stuck
In the fog, and they fuck.

He wishes he knew if he was hungry.
She wishes she knew if this was love.

Free Sex Chocolate

The three words that sell
Women's magazines
Are free, sex, and chocolate.

Of the three words that sell
Men's magazines
Two are different.

Anne Marie and I dream
Of a single magazine
Its pages are on fire.

We read it over
Each other's shoulder
And are consumed
        And are consumed
                And are consumed

The White

She scribbles the white out

      Her father praises the scribble
He thinks it's the poem.

She frowns.

The white is the poem, dada.

              She's right.

The white

Is the poem.

Blake and the Angels, Twice

I

Angels appear
At the Blakean ear
They whisper in there:

"You will become
The thing you despise
And then you will learn
To love it."

Blake grunts, and writes on.
Ezekial's song
Against tyrannous systems
Grows ever more rigorous
Intricate, disciplined
Until it completely
Controls and entraps
The lover of freedom
Who sings it.

II

Paralysed inside
The electric cage of his philosophy
Blake stares into the eyes
Of the angels
They have returned, as he dies
To console him.

He can see through their disguise
To their true disguise.
They are the wrong kind of angel.

He ignores them.

Audit, 1996

I have recorded my
Stallion profits

Indicated those benefits
Which were not at arm's length

Admitted the Name and Address of the person.
It was I who commenced
The Foreign Life Policy.

It's a year since I spoke to my brother
Desmond Richard Gough

Entertainment expenses
Cannot be recouped.

There will be no immediate repairs, or renewals.
Goodwill has been written off

Everything else is Other.

It Is Better To See Your Father Buried

It is better to see your father buried.
Neither Sylvia nor my mother did.
Their fathers walk away from them always
Strong-smelling and enormous.

Why don't they turn around?
Why don't they bend down, and kiss?

The Permanent Wave

She's saying goodbye
To her mother, to Ireland
– her father was dead by then –
Her arm is half-raised.

She has a new hairdo
To protect her, like armour.
Its curves are unyielding.
She's eighteen. Amazed.

You put down the photograph
What you are feeling
Rising within you
Will never go away.

Under the bridge
On which she is standing
Stands, vast and unnoticed
A permanent wave.

Philip

Intelligent, well-educated, in a new world of opportunity
He became minor by effort of will
Chose to live in Hull
On lino and the dull food of England.
For him, love never came off rationing
And he liked it like that.
You live longer half starving
And, once your metabolism's adjusted,
Too much makes you sick.

Girls From Leipzig Talk of Kurt Cobain

There's something about trams
And depression
And people talking German
That makes a guy want to write a poem.

Upstairs in Sankt Oberholz
The scattered poets at their laptops
Sigh and listen in, as girls
From Leipzig talk of Kurt Cobain

"Both his uncles killed themselves."
"It takes me longer when I'm sober."

Far below, the roadworks over
Trams grind onto Tor again.

Goal

They have installed the tiny goalposts
In the stand-up pissers
The tiny orange football
Is hanging by its thread,
Above the anti-splash mat,
Greener than the real grass.
Builders and philosophers
Blast it in the net.

Even when our cocks are out
It's football that we think about.

The final is on Sunday
At home, the wives are wet
They know that we have secrets
It's worse than they suspect.

This Page Intentionally Left Blank

Have an assignment on a poet, poem, or number of poems?

Don't even have a clue about how you should begin?

Remember, getting help is NOT the same as cheating.

You'd be foolish to try to
Complete your assignment
Without assistance.

Here's a tip: just because you use the words "mountains" and
"rivers" in your poem does not mean that they're going to
be in there. Those are just words. You have to do something
with them if you want to make poetry.

Pennsylvania residents, add 6% sales tax

For example.

Or you're writing a poem about a car. Fine.
Something needs to happen to the object.

Park it up my ass, why don'cha?

It's just a suggestion.

And always remember
If you're borrowing from Nietzsche
Staring into the void is
Void where prohibited by law.

Oh, this universe!
Subject to change without notice.

All rights reserved.
All rights reserved.
All rights reserved.

This page intentionally left blank.

Copyright Approximately, Inc.

To the extent possible
we have attempted to contact
current content copyright holders
for permission to reprint
or otherwise reproduce
those texts which are reproduced
on Plagiarist.

Plagiarist considers
its incoming e-mail
as a public forum,
and all material,
text,
binary data,
etcetera, etcetera,
sent to a Plagiarist.com
e-mail address
is the property of
Plagiarist.com.

Plagiarist may,
at its sole discretion,
publish any and all e-mail
sent to any Plagiarist address,
in whole or in part,
in perpetuity.

No delay or failure
to take action under
such terms and conditions
will constitute a waiver
by Plagiarist unless
expressly waived in writing
by a duly authorized
officer of Plagiarist
or Approximately, Inc.

Accordingly, you should
visit this website
from time to time to
review the then–current
and effective
terms and conditions
because they are binding on you.
Binding on you.
Binding on you.
Like vines of the forest
Binding on you.

All Plagiarist website design,
text,
images, buttons, icons, scripts,
etcetera, etcetera,
are copyrights of Plagiarist.

Don't steal our hard work.

Prince plays Creep at Coachella

Prince plays his red guitar and sings
"Creep" at Coachella
Halfway through
The song drops
Off a cliff
And all the listeners, left
Suspended
Gasp
And hold their breath.

In silence.

Till the band slams
Back into the ground of sound

And in that falling moment
I'm on the plane from Zagreb to Dubrovnik
As titanium falls
Engines and all

And all around me, water rises out of plastic glass, held tight
In sudden rising columns till the water strikes the ceiling lights
And then it falls like rain

The crowd shriek in the desert as Prince
Strikes his red guitar again

Black Ships

Oh Mother I don't want to come in from the garden
To change our pacific constitution

Oh darling it's different this time

Oh mother I don't want to refuel those black ships.
They are waking a butterfly in winter.

Thoughts on my Forty Second Birthday

I haven't wanted to be dead
For over a year.
Last week I got health insurance
For the first time in my life.

At this rate
I might even learn to drive.

Losing Your Perspective on the Berlin-Prague Express

Huge patches of big yellow flowers on a rough cliff face on the far side of the river

Mirror small patches of yellow lichen on the rough rocks passing by a few yards outside the train's other window.

There's a moment of fractal confusion as your brain decides they're on the same scale

And now when you glance back across the Elbe, it seems a trickle of water

About a foot wide

At the other side of which stand many tiny model houses

And incredibly lifelike cows the size of your thumb

And the model trees that rise up the steep polystyrene slopes seem shorter than the wild grasses that flick past the other window

As you look back again now, disoriented.

You make an effort to sort out the mistake

But your subconscious misunderstands the message

And the grasses become trees.

Mine

Poems are the landmines of the culture
One can lie dormant for decades
Deep in the stack of unopened books
Packed in the attic after your father
Died in the car, in the carpark, parking.

Then one day the boxes come down from the attic
For whatever reason, and you open
The wrong one, and
Bang.

Another man is lying on the floor, sobbing, unable to breathe.

Gold

You will be leaving your children
The date will be set
Memorise their changing faces
Atoms blow to their appointed places
The roof will fall on all these houses
Don't forget to snap their seatbelts tight.

Everything beautiful is turned into money
Everything true is turned into money
Everything that you cannot own is turned into money
Everything that cannot be sold is turned into money
Debt is turned into money
Bread is turned into money
Paper is turned into money
All that is solid turns into money
All that is money melts into air

Poets complain about copyright theft

And King Midas touches your beautiful children
Still in their seatbelts
As soon as the car's out of sight.

Oh it's too late to change my name
And now I have nowhere to hide.
The situation isn't clear until it's too late.
I used to lean forward into the mike
Lately, I lean back.

I want to see my daughter but she's in another house
And she's asleep
And she's been turned into gold.

Spilt Lemonade

Anthony sings Bob Dylan
Over the credits, at the end of the film
Knocking on Heaven's Door

The film ends
The song ends
The lights come on
Everybody's gone

I am there, ankle-deep in silence
Waiting for the film to begin
A man comes in,
Holding up a rubbish bin
(Will there be sex? And violence?)
He picks up wrappers of the things consumed
And asks me if I have a ticket
Tears it in two.
Leaves, and the thick door
Closes with a soft suck
Like a kiss in a dream
Like an airlock
In a submarine.

The speakers pour a low fizz through the room
Like spilt lemonade
Dying all around me on the floor.

Austrian Airlines

The Austrian girl that I kissed
While writing my book in Cadíz
Made such a big fuss
About what to do next
I got bored and wandered off.

Years later, that memory – click.

As I enter the sinister Disney
Of Austrian Airlines
Air hostesses in red shoes
Red tights
Red skirts
Red tops
As the same Strauss waltzes play again and again
And again, and will never stop.
The doors close.
The hostesses switch off
The heat and electricity of their
Red lipstick smiles.

I wonder will the smoke of our flesh blend
After falling a strong mile.

Dromineer, December 2007

I

A winter storm has thatched the east shore of Lough Derg
In the traditional manner, by breaking
All last year's dead reeds across the knee of the wind,
Then waves – chop-chop – chivvy ten thousand tons of them
Across the lake and into position
Interlocked along seventy miles of shore.

Today, the obsessive-compulsive waves have
Calmed down a bit, but
Still fiddle with it every few seconds
Like Christo and Jeanne-Claude
Adjusting the raw silk hem of an island,
Unable to drag themselves away.
Like a writer at Christmas, poking a poem
Trying to enjoy the break
Unable to enjoy the break
Trying to enjoy the break
From writing.

II

The sun makes a grudging appearance
For one minute, to two shivering fans
Who've been standing on the concrete jetty in the rain.
"That'll have ta do ye."
It ducks back behind the zinc clouds
And sinks fast below the black hills.

"Fuck this, I'm off back to Australia,"
Mumbles one of the fans, or the sun.

It's hard to tell over the
Splash of the lake waves, the
Crash of the lakeside
Property prices, the
Crying of developers and birds.

American Haiku

Ten thousand syllables

A break

Thirty thousand syllables

A break

Bashō applauds, but it's not over.

We will be back with
A hundred thousand great new
Syllables, after

This break.

I Think Continually Of Those Who Were Really Something (I)

I think continually of those who were really something
Creating a small universe every couple of years
Many of which continue to function
Receiving ambassadors, tourists and Vandals
Who, unfamiliar with the concept of stairs,
Walk through the squares, staring into doorways
Entirely unaware of the upper stories.

"It's alright, but he can't hold a candle to
Andy McNab" "…Cecelia Ahern."

Behind them, high and unobserved
A single light, incandescent
Continues to burn.

City, star and satellite.

Stadt, Satellit, und Stern.

I Think Continually Of Those Who Were Really Something (II)

I think continually of those who were really something.
Spontaneously combusting, in a locked room,
Their fat burning, bones thinning
Hair, gums and memories receding
Till suddenly there's nothing left
But a corpse and a pile of books.

I say goodbye, lock the door.
Settle into the chair.

I Think Continually Of Those Who Were Really Something (III)

I think continually of those who were really something
They hang around, watching me not write
As I sit selfish on a train
And a woman stands, caught between the age
When men stand for beauty, and the age
When men stand for age.

Later, on a plane, I trade my night's sleep for the poem
And drink a late coffee to sharpen my brain
In the hope of nailing something in the last lines
To justify the day.

Later still, about to land,
I think:
It's not even a good poem
And I made her stand

Embers

The embers of Bristol glow orange through thin cloud
Orange, too, the headrest cloths on this Easyjet plane
(Orange, too, the flame.)

But she lands OK
The city is bright with sodium light
Corpses wake in the long rows
And fill slowly with their names.

I Like These Empty Hours

I like these empty hours
Bristol airport, Luton, Stanstead
Orly, Schoenefeld, Dublin, Tegel
Belfast, Shannon, here

Looking up from a good book to be
Surprised by which side of the clouds I'm on
Both phones off between time zones.

Then sodium light and slight delays
A shuttle bus on a concrete apron
A smell of jet fuel, and men suppressing fear

Sometimes something flowers
Blasting dogshit off a shoesole in a hotel shower

Plymouth

For the whores of Plymouth
Nothing changes but the drug
Beer, then gin, then opium.
Heroin. Temazepam
Its benzodiazepine
Will get you to sleep early
Now that cutbacks in the Fleet
Mean you don't do overtime.

The terraced cliffs are silent in November
And the forts and guns
Grow self-conscious in the peace.
All enemies asleep.

The Beatles lie on Plymouth Hoe
Ringo points towards the sea.

The Summer We All Grew Up

I recall kissing
You and your brothers
Among others

The summer we all grew up

I recall kissing
Your genitalia
Inter alia

The summer we all grew up

And looking back we were babies
Who thought they were world weary
Everyone caught scabies
And called each other dearie

The summer we all grew up.

You Will Believe A Man Can Fly

He faked his way
Through the interview
By doing shitloads of cocaine.

His flatmate was a DJ
Gave it to him, as a present
And told him what to do.

"Vivacious", two of the panel wrote.
"Loud," wrote the third. In caps.
He'd spent the next day in bed quietly sobbing.

Getting the job almost renewed the high.

Now he's a week into it, and back to normal.

He stands in the aisle and twangs the elastic
Of the facemask, three times.

A big, wobbly pudding of a man.

He twangs it so hard it snaps.

Fields

The field-shapes of the city blocks
London's paddocks, and a meadow, perhaps.
New York's gridded eastern fields, the vaster gridded prairies of LA.
Rio's unfenced clearcut jungle of favela sweeping over treeless hills
The terraced vineyards facing south
In Sicilian cities hugging bays.

What is mediaeval Galway but
A slinky mesh of limestone walls
And ever littler limestone walls
That cut across a limestone floor.
And through it all, a cattle path.

Shop Street's hot with shoppers
Shopping. Out to see the sales.

And, out to sea, the sails.

Inside

Soft scrape. I look over.
Nails on paper.
Sophie is trying to pick up
Something in the corner
Of a picture
In a book.
She looks over
"Get in book?"
My daughter
Walks on water
At right angles to fiction.
Her heels on sand and toes in sky.
She grabs the sides of the book and tries
To climb inside.

Closed Loop

I

You can only astonish them once.

Afterwards, to your surprise
You find that you are still alive

Bringing better and better work
To a smaller and smaller audience.

II

You enter the valley of the post-structuralists
Everywhere their guns, magnificent
Point straight down, or straight up
Innovative, revolutionary, and useless.

III

The poems you wrote were spare and unpeopled.
Nobody cared.
You weren't writing for them.
You weren't writing for you.
The process continued. Usually at night.
Semi-automatic, like gunfire
Or ivy climbing a dead tree.

IV

Inconvenient and absurd
Words which cannot be sold
Continue to emerge
At night keeping you awake
Like stigmata, or flatulence

Selfless and selfish,
Speaking only of themselves.
Eventually you don't even bother to turn on the light.
They pile up on top of each other
Like industrial products without an industry
Ghosts of something we don't need.

Not even the thing itself.

Seven Fake Zen Poems

I

Here we go, again.
Another drawing of a pen.

II

Here we go, again
Fake zen
Is still zen.

III

Here we go
Again
Go we here

IV

Look
A mountain
How amusing

V

Look
A volcano
How amusing

VI

Look
My death
How amusing

VII

Look
Amusement
How amusing

Episode C-49

I sit
Having a shit
In a toilet on the first floor
Of Media Factory Berlin.
I'm due to re-record two lines
As the home-made son of Frankenstein
In episode C-49
Of "Lily the Witch", at half past five.
(The Canadians object to the word "girlfriend"
And to the phrase "Your hair looks beautiful in the moonlight".)

There has been a delay
Due to an unspecified technical glitch.
I take a break.
Then this awkward poem arrives.
Broken in the middle.
I write it down, sighing, pants round my ankles.

Elsewhere, men sell machines
For punching holes in other human beings.
Study zen, my ass.
We accept all things already.
We just don't know it yet.

Phone

We negotiate on the phone
She doesn't like the word
Cunt.
I suggest pussy
She thinks a little.
I can hear her breathing
And I can hear the phone breathing

(The electronic breath
Of early mobile phones
This is years ago)

Pussy turns out to be good.
I do most of the talking
As usual.
I tell her what I'd like to be doing
And she tells me what she's doing

She likes fiction
And I like truth
So this turns out pretty good.

(I make up stories for love and for a living
It makes me impatient with other people's fictions
I can see the imperfections
I want to go and fix them
It's very distracting.
But other people's truths
I can handle
In unlimited amounts.
Especially when
Gasped by women.

Carpenters hate tables, but they love trees.)

It took a long time
Because she'd been drinking.
I had to hold back
In order to join her
Where she wanted to be joined
In the place where words
Are impossible and unnecessary
In the animal heaven
Where I am unemployed.

Streetlight came in the window
Of someone else's office.
All of this accomplished
On someone else's phone bill
(This was once upon a time
A long time ago
When phone calls cost a lot of dosh)

I lay on the floor
After she'd hung up
My cheek to the pine board.
Lost in the pale wood.

Sophie on Max Beer Strasse

Today was a good day
See Sophie run
She had eat
She had many fun.

Rewind the sun
Sophie is one.
Rewind the sun
Sophie is gone.

Rewind the sun
An identical girl
Dies in the arms
Of her mother
The cries of her aunts
Smother the guns.

The key in which they sing
Is the real thing.

And afterward, all of the songs
From hymns to hit singles
Have somehow gone wrong.

Bob the Builder
Can he fix it?
No he can't.

Zzzzzzzzzz

Jazz Jews throwing rocks at
Jazz Muslims throwing rocks at
Jazz Christians throwing rocks at
Jazz Jews throwing rocks at
Jazz Christians throwing rocks at
Jazz Muslims throwing rocks at
Jazz Jews.
The rocks are made out of rock
This makes them heavy
And they are tired now.
They fall asleep in the quarry
And dream of Jazzzzzzzzzzzzzzzzzzzzzzzzzzzzzzzzzzzzzzzzzzzzzzz
zzzzzzzzzzzzzzzzzzzzzzzzzzzzzzzzzzzzzzzzzzzzzzzzzzzzzzzzzzzzzzzz
zzzzzzzzzzzzzzzzzzzzzzzzzzzzzzzzzzzzzzzzzzzzzzzzzzzzzzzzzzzzzzzz
zzzzzzzzzzzzzzzzzzzzzzzzzzzzzzzzzzzzzzzzzzzzzzzzzzzzzzzzzzzzzzzz
zzzzzzzzzzzzzzzzzzzzzzzzzzzzzzzzzzzzzzzzzzzzzzzzzzzzzzzzzzzzzzzz
zzzzzzzzzzzzzzzzzzzzzzzzzzzzzzzzzzzzzzzzzzzzzzzzzzzzzzzzzzzzzzzz
zzzzzzzzzzzzzzzzzzzzzzzzzzzzzzzzzzzzzzzzzzzzzzzzzzzzzzzzzzzzzzzz
zzzzzzzzzzzzzzzzzzzzzzzzzzzzzzzzzzzzzzzzzzzzzzzzzzzzzzzzzzzzzzzz
zzzzzzzzzzzzzzzzzzzzzzzzzzzzzzzzzzzzzzzzzzzzzzzzzzzzzzzzzzzzzzzz
zzzzzzzzzzzzzzzzzzzzzzzzzzzzzzzzzzzzzzzzzzzzzzzzzzzzzzzzzzzzzzzz
zzzzzzzzzzzzzzzzzzzzzzzzzzzzzzzzzzzzzzzzzzzzzzzzzzzzzzzzzzzzzzzz
zzzzzzzzzzzzzzzzzzzzzzzzzzzzzzzzzzzzzzzzzzzzzzzzzzzzzzzzzzzzzzzz
zzzzzzzzzzzzzzzzzzzzzzzzzzzzzzzzzzzzzzzzzzzzzzzzzzzzzzzzzzzzzzzz
zzzzzzzzzzzzzzzzzzzzzzzzzzzzzzzzzzzzzzzzzzzzzzzzzzzzzzzzzzzzzzzz
zzzzzzzzzzzzzzzzzzzzzzzzzzzzzzzzzzzzzzzzzzzzzzzzzzzzzzzzzzzzzzzz
zzzzzzzzzzzzzzzzzzzzzzzzzzzzzzzzzzzzzzzzzzzzzzzzzzzzzzzzzzzzzzzz
zzzzzzzzzzzzzzzzzzzzzzzzzzzzzzzzzzzzzzzzzzzzzzzzzzzzzzzzzzzzzzzz
zzzzzzzzzzzzzzzzzzzzzzzzzzzzzzzzzzzzzzzzzzzzzzzzzzzzzzzzzzzzzzzz
zzzzzzzzzzzzzzzzzzzzzzzzzzzzzzzzzzzzzzzzzzzzzzzzzzzzzzzzzzzzzzzz
zzzzzzzzzzzzzzzzzzzzzzzzzzzzzzzzzzzzzzzzzzzzzzzzzzzzzzzzzzzzzzzz
zzzzzzzzzzzzzzzzzzzzzzzzzzzzzzzzzzzzzzzzzzzzzzzzzzzzzzzzzzzzzzzz.

A Brief Final Message From The Jomon People, About Whom I Know Nothing

We buried our kings on the Tokyo plain
Well, we won't be doing that again
Goodbye, goodbye, goodbye

Poems from The Psychedelian:

THE ANOREXIC BODY-BUILDER

If I'm very lucky, once a year
(Maybe twice, if I've been eating fish)
I am dazzled by a bright idea
And here's the one I got this year (I wish
It was a bit more bright, but it's bright-ish)
Anyway, yes, body-building, then.
It's an anorexia for men.

All the girls I know hate body-builders,
Find the mass of rippling flesh disgusting
Certainly not sexy. It bewilders
Boys to think their sister could be thrusting
Fingers down her throat like that... No lusting
After bulk for women then. And mannish
Boys have no desire at all to vanish.

To blow the self up, and to disappear:
Two expressions of a single urge
To shout the Will and make the body hear.
The body-builder wills the flesh to surge
The anorexic wills an ebb, a purge
The Stalin of the mind lets the tanks roll:
The body is a place they can control

Each pursues a lunatic ideal
Each is lonely in the mad pursuit
When the vision of oneself's unreal
The vision of all others lacks a root
The muscle-man exploding through his suit
The wisp of girl who frowns at her reflection
They both recede from us toward Perfection.

This should end with some kind of conclusion.
Final statement. Answer to the riddle.
If I could, I'd give you the solution
Or at least some figures you could fiddle
But I can't, I'm stuck here in the middle
Seeing men expand and women shrink
I watch them go, and don't know what to think.

(*From* The Psychedelian, Issue 3 Volume 1, Thursday Oct. 21st, 1994)

THE FASHION COLUMN

Fashion has been on my mind of late
As I stride down Shop Street in my splendour
I myself am fashion incarnate
But there's a girl who wears what Oxfam send her
And look, he's passed his wardrobe through a blender...
One cannot tell the children of the wealthy
From the wino, which I think is healthy.

There is something very democratic
About an age in which the youthful dress
Is less a statement, bold, clear-cut, emphatic
And more a kind of accidental mess
History will be kind to us, I'd guess.
You didn't see the Hitler Youth in baggies
With hair and clothes like Scooby-Doo and Shaggy's.

Fashion as an industry appals me
A jacket or a skirt don't stop being good
The day after some couture hemlines fall, be-
Cause John Galliano says they should.
Christ, if I have rightly understood
Who wore a cheap robe, didn't eff and blind it
When he found out Ghost had not designed it.

Thus I hope you won't think I am joking
If I call this fashion's Golden Age
Though I'm passing, lately, through a smoking
Jacket, silk shirt, cufflink kind of stage
I celebrate the scruff that's all the rage.
Wearing other people's clothes with pride
May not keep us safe from genocide
(Bug and bomb aren't easily outwitted)
But, I hope, we're less sure to commit it.

(*From* The Psychedelian, Issue 2 Volume 1, Thursday Oct. 14th, 1994)

THE DRUG COLUMN

Did you notice National Anti-Drug Week?
Wasn't it the greatest pile of shite?
Froth and nonsense spouted by a smug geek
Who wouldn't know hashish from Marlboro Light
And all those Dublin actors every night
On 2FM, "Yeah, drugs, I took so many
I went mad, and blind, and robbed my granny."

By mixing up a brew of truth and lies
They took away the good they could have done
Painting "pot" as Satan in disguise
Couldn't fool an old, teetotal nun
People take this stuff because it's fun
If you say "An E makes you feel bad"
The kids reply (quite rightly): you've been had.

It is true that "drugs" are wrecking Finglas
Tallaght, half of Dublin, but what's new?
If it wasn't smack it would be Guinness
If it wasn't that it would be glue

These are guys with nothing else to do
Take away the smack and crack and hash
And they'd be buying Vim for ready cash

It's madness, making taking drugs a crime
What we smoke, snort, or inject our butt with
Is our business: kids die all the time
Not from "drugs" but from the stuff it's cut with
Prisons fill: you couldn't fill a hut with
Those "improved" or "cured" by sharing cells
With rapists, thieves and other ne'er-do-wells.
Legalise it, save a generation
Let them all receive this from their nation:
A chance to gently get out of their head
And not end up a criminal, or dead.

(*From* The Psychedelian, Issue 4 Volume 1, Thursday Oct. 28th, 1994)

LETTER TO MY KIDS

Hullo kids, I know you're not born yet
But here I am in nineteen ninety four
The summer number one's been Wet Wet Wet
Just like the weather, lordy what a bore
I don't know why I live here any more
(I've not yet met your mother to my knowledge
Although I may, who knows, next week in college)

Summer having ended with a whimper
Galway undergoes the usual change
Tourists hobble home (their wallets limper)
To be swapped for students in a strange
Parody of a hostage exchange:
We send their useless buskers packing home
And take back thirty thousand of our own

Incidentally, what do buskers do
In the towns where they were born and bred
Would they, could they, have the gall to screw
Pennies from their old assistant head
a passing aunt, their mother, cousin Fred?
No, they're right to travel far each year.
At home they'd get a clip around the ear.

Rain and buskers, students, Wet Wet Wet
What a catalogue of horror this is
It is easy sometimes to forget
That Galway misses, if indeed it misses,
Perfection by a thin slice of iced kisses.
(Dear old Galway's fine if you forgive her
Odd habit of shitting in her river.)

I do hope you'll enjoy this pre-birth present
My charming unborn Egbert and Amelia
I must say writing it is jolly pleasant
(Although of course this newsletter is really a
Sort of jumped-up ad for PSYCHEDELIA
I know Steve who runs the club, you see
And, being handsome, I am let in free)

(*From* The Psychedelian, Issue 1 Volume 1, Thursday Oct. 7th, 1994)

Part 2: SONGS

Songs for Swinging Celibates

(Toasted Heretic, 1988)

Sodom Tonight

It's so nasty out there, it's perfectly horrid
People walk around with numbers on their forehead
All of the prophets are moving out of town
The lambs are being slaughtered as the abattoir falls down

Well, we'll have to spend tomorrow in Gomorrah
But baby, Sodom tonight

Oh all the dirty bookshops are full of revelations
They're crucifying winos in the railway stations
Mouths full of dust, they've got eyes full of mud
Deep down town they're turning whiskey into blood

A guy with holes in his hands, waving a Bible
Runs under our window, naked, screaming 'Libel!'
The whore on the corner has her red dress on,
Back from a weekend with her mother in Babylon

Well the bread's turned to rock in the bread-bin
It's getting dark awful early, shall I turn on the light?
Well, we're gonna have to spend tomorrow in Gomorrah,
Begorrah, but baby Sodom tonight.

Very Naughty Party

Ah, weirdos and thickos & bigots & wackos
On smack and on crack and on Balkan tobaccos
Giving hand jobs in toilets and head on the stairs
Wall to wall mattress and there aren't any chairs
They haven't any Pepsi and I've lost my comb
This is a very naughty party and I think I'll go home.

Very naughty party…
This is a very naughty party…
This is a very naughty party
And I wanna go home

The music is loud and dreadfully depressing
Young ladies in black are slowly undressing
Young boys mumble lines like "I've nothing to lose"
Sniff Ajax and sneeze and then puke on their shoes
I can't bear to see scenes of such degradation
So I turn my attention to the girl and Alsatian…

This is a very naughty party
And I wanna go home

Children these days, I just don't understand
As I'm trapped by a girl who drums in a band
I merely asked quite politely for a small glass of water
She must have misheard… if she were my daughter…
What on earth is she doing, the excesses of Rome
Have nothing on this, Christ I'd better go home

This is a very naughty party
And I wanna go home

How she can do that with only one hand
Is something I'll never ever ever understand
And what on earth is he doing, why he could be my double
Oh dear, it's a mirror, I'm in serious trouble
The floor is unspeakable, the ceiling is scummy
I can't take any more, beam me up mummy…

This is a very naughty party
And I wanna go home

Galway Bay

Well, I'm in the Bay City and I'm sitting pretty pretty
And you're pretty pretty and you're sitting on me
And I'm pretty witty and you're itty bitty
And isn't it a pity the city can't see?

The sun goes down on Galway Bay
The daughter goes down on me
Her dad's not due till one or maybe two
And I'm as happy as I'll ever be

You're so cute in your birthday suit
And I'm so cool in mine
I could play all day with your exotic fruit
If you didn't have school at nine

The sun goes down on Galway Bay
The daughter goes down on me
Her dad's not due till one or maybe two
And I'm as happy as I'll ever be

I'm the kind of boy that fits into your bed
You give me everything I ever wanted
You're the kind of girl that fits into my bed
I'll give you everything you ever wanted

The sun goes down on Galway Bay
The daughter goes down on me
Her dad's not due till one or maybe two
And I'm as happy as I'll ever be...

Black Contact Lenses

All you ever wanted was to
Write a song as perfect as
"Take The Skinheads Bowling", but
Of course you never did.
Ah, you would have settled for
A lifetime in that lover
Who swapped you for another and
Much inferior kid.

You lost most of your money and your
Tan and your muscles
On your last trip to Brussels with
Your Italian pet
And you didn't get laid
And you didn't get paid
And you haven't even made a good
Song of it yet

And all the words she wrote to you
Were spelt wrong or were lies
And she bought black contact lenses when
You said you liked her eyes.

And all the words she wrote to you
Were spelt wrong or were lies
And she bought black contact lenses when
You said you liked her eyes.

Goodbye to Berlin

If I close my eyes, you know, everything goes away
If I close my eyes again, it could be Berlin, 1928

We're discussing Isherwood, isn't he good?
In my faggotty hat I chat of this and that.
I'm talking 'bout Stephen Spender
People say that I'm a bender
I don't like cigarettes or beer
It's obvious I'm queer.

Well goodbye to all that
Gonna get me some muscles
Gonna get me some fat
Well, goodbye to all that
Goodbye to Berlin

I'm sick and tired of people swearing
At me 'cause of what I'm wearing
I've heard enough of what people say
Why don't they mind their business anyway?
I'm going to get me some army boots
And a three-piece suit, yeah
A three-piece suit.
I'm going to kick the living shit
Out of anyone who laughs at it, oh
I'll push your face in, if your face annoys
If your face annoys.
I'm a-gonna be, I'm a-gonna be
One of the boys...

Well goodbye to all that
Gonna get me some muscles
Gonna get me some fat
Well, goodbye to all that
Goodbye to Berlin

Love Theme from "Yeats: The Movie"

Put another pint of acid in
The battery of hate
You're the one
I really want
To mutilate.

Still Life With Girl

She said, "I've wasted God's time with my petty requests
I've called upon demons to settle my debts
Now angels are screaming across my sky
Angels are screaming and I know why
And I
And I
Just can't get enough sleep at night."
She said
She said
"I'd hoped my life
Would just fall into place
But…
Not this place."
She said, "All those years I knew
That I was doing something wrong."
I said, "Don't I know you
From a Lloyd Cole song?"
And she said "Ah…"
And she said
"Ah…"

Bouncing Off The Boulders

She waited for me once
Beneath a dead tree
To tell me by moonlight
She'd never loved me.
I was surprised, though I should have
Suspected as much
Since she'd stolen my wheelchair
And broken my crutch

And as she dumped my body
Over the cliff
I said to myself
"I wonder if..."
I said to myself
As I began to descend
"I wonder if this
Could perhaps be the end?"

I wondered aloud
As I bounced off the boulders
"Has the burden of love
Been removed from my shoulders?"
I pondered aloud
As I bled on the sand
"What's she trying to say here?
I don't understand."

I said to myself
As my blood stained the sea
"Now what could it be...
That she's saying to me?"

The Best Things In Life Are Mine

The spirit is weak, so she adds a little vodka
Goes to bed, perchance to sleep
Counts the men
Who've been there, then
She counts the cost.
Pretty cheap.
She murmurs, "Everything I touch
Turns to me and says
Can I stay?"
She says "I feel fine
The best things in life are mine."
She says "God I'm wrecked."
She is perfectly correct.

She says,
"And sometimes... I feel so young
And sometimes... I feel like this
But the best things in life are mine
Oh yes."

She says "I feel fine
The best things in life are mine."
She says "God I'm wrecked."
She is perfectly correct.

Charm & Arrogance

(Toasted Heretic, 1989)

Drown the Browns

Their mother had children and, thinking she should,
She attempted to love them, but my God who could?
Kill your children, Mrs. Brown
Do your bit for Tidy Town
Remove your white trash from the gutter
Melt your sons for soap and butter

And every time I take a bath
I'll think of Malachi, and laugh
And I'll recall each punch and boast
As I spread Martin on my toast.
Drown the Browns

Their father had squatters' rights in three prisons
Their mother, when conscious, could not make decisions
Imbibers of cider and pre-teen joy-riders
Sharpening screwdrivers, as I made a glider
Which they later smashed, in woodwork class
They stole all the tools but they still didn't pass.

Drown the Browns

Lost and Found

Got an album and a book I wanted,
Look around, everybody's haunted
By the thought that nobody will miss them,
Ah, I just want to kiss them.
Hate their jobs and hate themselves,
Little bottoms stuck to shelves
Nobody will ever love them
But I think highly of them.

Here is contrast, here is variety
Here are the necessary evils of society.
I am pride, they are shame
In their garden, it shall always rain.
I am arrogance, they are mock humility
It has come to pass, their opinion of their ability.

I've been lost and I've been found
Wandering the underground…

I got on a train to get out of the rain
And I found a girl like me
I am happy as a tree, I have found a girl like me
We have arrogance and charm,
These people cannot do us harm
How they hate us, how they scowl
Laying it on with a trowel.
La la la la la…
Laying it out on a tea tray
How they fibrillate when we say
La la la la la la lah…

I've been lost and I've been found
Wandering the underground.

LSD (isn't what it used to be)

The sun pours down like honey
Like money
Like rain
The boy who took the credit
Is the boy to blame.
On your three-figure mushroom debut
Heaven knows what got into you
Did he turn to liquid too?
I don't want to know.

LSD isn't what it used to be
You're growing tiresome and I'm growing up
Listen sometime to the useless things you say
Why don't you listen sometime?

We have known each other
Since we were ten
I'm too tired
To begin again.
I never believed in love
I once believed in you
You called me uncool.
How true.

LSD isn't what it used to be
You're growing tiresome and I'm growing up
Listen sometime to the useless, hurtful things you say
Why don't you listen, sometime?

Stay Tonight

May all your Christmases be pleasant
May you dine on venison and pheasant
May you munch on meaty vegetarian
May all your uncles be Hungarian,
Hey hey hey,
And may your life be good.

May your diplomatic fool boyfriend,
Distinguished member of the motor-pool, oh man,
Fade away,
Hey hey hey,
And may your life be good.

There's plenty boyfriends in the sea, so spend tonight with me
Oh, stay tonight, I invite you to
Woooooh, ooooh-uh-oooh oooh

You're cool, you're free
Hang on to me
You're sweet, you're bright
So stay tonight
I invite you to.
May you have the sense to see
That you should be with me
If not eternally
Then let me see,
At least till three
And should you miss
Your bus at four...

Well you know there's plenty more
Buses in the sea, so spend tonight with me
Oh stay tonight, I invite you to,
Woooooh, ooooh-uh-oooh oooh
There's plenty boyfriends in the sea, so spend tonight with me

Oh stay tonight, I invite you to
Stay tonight.
Stay tonight.
Stay tonight.

You Make Girls Unhappy

She looked at you, walked past, and asked the next stranger directions
Contrary to your belief, girls don't just want erections
You make girls unhappy

You've got all the girls money can buy
It's fewer than you expected, why?
'cause you make girls unhappy

Stockbrokers want to break your stocks
Oxfam will not feed your ox
Aunties knee you in the rocks
'cause you make girls unhappy.

Abandon the Galleries

Now that art is a game designed to bring
Wealth and fame to wealthy and famous investors
How sad if perhaps it should collapse
On the startled heads of these poor bastards.

Midday sunflowers, starry night
Cue taxfree corporate delight
Buy now, last few remaining
In Gainsborough, everybody's gaining.
Abandon the galleries.

But should there be no further bids
And should rich men cease to believe
All they'll be left with is paint on some canvases
A room full of art, and a heart full of grief.
Protect the rich from plunging prices
Existential midlife crisis
Protect the collectors from their art
Protect the collectors.

Abandon the galleries.

Here Comes the New Year

Here comes the new year
Oh no, not again
I've been playing Ziggy with my friends
Neither keen on dying nor on being bored
A year of careful hand-stands
On the high-board.

Don't want to get up,
I'm tired of everything
I've watched the pornographic film
And worn the wedding ring
The kitchen's full of food I do not want to see
Downstairs, there's a letter for me.

Things to be and things to do
Nothing that I want to
Read a book or write my own
I fumble with a telephone
Wish that I was not alone
My little girl is far from home
Here comes the new year.

I talk too much, I bore my friends
I bore myself, then bore my friends again

Here comes the new year.

There Goes Everything

She's a cancer in my bed.
She's a cancer in my bed.
"I cannot answer," she said.

And so we listen
To the silence ring.

There
Goes everything.

Go To Sleep

Running up and down
Wearing uncle's crown
You are the sun
To almost everyone
Amongst the pines
Your father gives you wine
It is summertime
It is always summertime…

You're lonely and drunk
The boats of your hopes have sunk
You're sick with self-pity and old photographs.
Go to sleep.

Lying on the beach
With nothing out of reach
Your mother kisses you
And offers you a peach
It's a beautiful day
In a beautiful town
You laugh aloud
You're blonde and brown…

You're lonely and drunk
The boats of your hopes have sunk
You're sick with self-pity and old photographs.
Go to sleep.

Floating on the water
Of the deep blue pool
Dutiful daughter
Beautiful fool
It never lasts forever
Those films lied.
You never even tried.

You're lonely and drunk
The boats of your hopes have sunk
You're sick with self-pity and old photographs.
Go to sleep.

Charm & Arrogance

Very broad of shoulder, slightly less of mind
Here is the boy she left behind
His the behind she left before she met me... honestly.

And he says "Hey!" and I say "What?"
And he says, "Whatcha got that I ain't got?"
And I say "Pardon?" and he says "Hey!
What's she see in you anyway?"

And I say, "Well, I'm sexy as hell,
I'm an excellent lover and reasonable cook
She likes my wit and the way that I spit
And she adores the narratorial voice of my book.
Her love of my lyrics is only surpassed
By her great admiration for my vocal inflections
She approves of my charity, complexional clarity
Dress sense, intelligence, all-day erections.
Delights in my habit of quoting from Nabokov
Can't get enough of my Old World gentility
Thinks that my sketches of local letches
Show an exceptional technical facility
Found it charming that on my disarming
A recent intruder at four in the morning
I fined him his trousers, wallet and gun
Let him off with a warning, and forgot to tell anyone.

Some, if not all, of these characteristics
Lead to her lipstick's being on me."

Some Drugs

Some drugs make you funky, some drugs make you twitch
Some drugs take your money and some drugs make you rich
Some drugs raise revenue, some drugs don't
Some drugs will do anything, some drugs won't

Some drugs make you better, some drugs make you worse
Some drugs lead to half completed dream-induced romantic verse
Some drugs give you pain, some drugs cure it
Some drugs give you so much pleasure you just can't endure it

Some drugs take your money, some drugs give it back
Some drugs make you so damn beautiful, some drugs turn your
    teeth black
Some drugs kill your cancers, some drugs give you worse ones
You can get some drugs in public houses, and more drugs when
    the nurse comes

Some drugs make you handsome, some drugs killed your mother
People tend to have some, one way or another
Some drugs make you ugly, just look at your father
They may say they love you, but you know they'd rather some drugs

You Can Always Go Home

Beware of your dreams,
They just might come true
Oh, these are wild wild times
As what I wanted turns to what I do
And I am king of nursery rhymes.

You can always
Go home.

You can always go home
If I'm really so bad,
If I'm really so cold,
You can always go home.

Beware of your dreams,
They just might come true
Oh, these are wild wild times
As what I wanted turns to what I do
And I am king of nursery rhymes.

The Smug EP
(Toasted Heretic, 1990)

Don't You Wish You Were Good?

I know you're asleep
That's why I can speak
You're my beautiful girl
And you're so weak
Don't you wish you were good?
I sometimes do
Yes I wish you were good
Well, it's something to do

I should leave
I know I should
Stupid to ask
But don't you wish you were good?
Don't you wish you were?

Can you feel my breath
In your hair
In your dreams
Down there
Will you ever change?

I should leave
I know I should
Stupid to ask
But don't you wish you were good?
Don't you wish you were?

Sun Says Hi

I get out of bed
Kiss your breast
Pull on a shirt and wander downstairs
Blinking in the sunlight in the kitchen,
Pick up an apple and walk into the garden.

Crazy with bees, breeze in the trees
I look up and I watch you dress
It's lovely while it lasts.
Sun says hi, and I say yes.

I lie on the grass, cools my back
Happy in the moment, it's a useful knack
Close my eyes and think of nothing
Through my eyelids, orange sunshine.

From the house now comes some music
In this moment I am perfect
Safe and calm and warm and free
Days like this will fit no diary.

Crazy with bees, breeze in the trees
I look up and I watch you dress
It's lovely while it lasts.
Sun says hi, and I say yes.

They Didn't Teach Music In My School

When your calls go uncollected
And your neighbours have electrified the fence
When will you start thinking, will it sink in,
Will you exercise some sense?
Everybody hates you, thinks it's great you've got the flu,
Do you know why?

It's because you're such a shite they'll laugh all night
With sheer delight the day you die.
Your hand inside your habit, you would grab it
And emit a gasping noise
As you walked in your black cassock past the showers
And slapped the buttocks of the boys.

But we got out alive
We're rich, we're famous
And you're inside for sliding up Seamus.

In our religion classes you would glare through black-rimmed glasses
Down the back
And summon up the sinner who'd regurgitated dinner
To be smacked
Vomiting in terror was a tactical error, he'd find
As you lowered his trews and began to bruise his behind.
Picture our joy when you were caught inside a boy behind the bike shed
Oh, summer holidays forever and much better weather when you're dead.

But we got out alive
We're rich, we're famous
And you're still inside for sliding up Seamus.

Amen.

Let's Get Drunk

There's solace in drink and a drink in your hand
All the culture you can eat, all the yoghurt you can understand
Our dancing around each other has grown too intricate
Let's get drunk, uncoordinated and inarticulate

You're not the young lady I want tonight
Let's get drunk and fight.

There is a tax on ignorance
It runs at twelve percent
You shouldn't have signed those documents
Till you knew what they meant

You gotta have rain in a lovesong
You've got to have pain in your voice
Convention demands it, baby
You ain't got no choice

You're not the young lady I want tonight
Let's get drunk and fight.

Another Day, Another Riot

(Toasted Heretic, 1992)

Unrealistic

In this terrible disco, in this terrible town
I want to hug you, and slap them around
Your lecherous cousin, your treacherous aunt
With her bitter little comments on the way you dance
It's somebody's birthday, the gang's all here
Every rotten relative rigid with beer
Celebrating someone else who didn't escape this year
They're always telling you, be realistic
But look what that got them
Nine kids, black eyes, cheap lipstick

Unrealistic, I want you to be
Unrealistic, look at me
The unrealistic life can be heavenly
Be unrealistic, but honestly
Unrealistic, just look at me
Unrealistic. Won't you look at me?

The fathers of friends of ours,
Having hated work for thirty years,
Retire, in time to die of cancer.
Never put it off. Not the important stuff.
These last three years I've had nothing
And all the time I've been pursuing everything
And I have been
As happy as I've ever been
But I have heard death, heard him giggle and chortle
As friends postponed pleasures as though they're immortal…

Another Day, Another Riot

Another day, another riot
Burn the banks and burn the bills
People like you can't keep quiet
People like me don't get ill
We just die
At three or four in the morning
We just die
We don't get to see the dawn.

Another day, another riot
Stuck in fog again
Will I always be this lucky?
Will you always be my friend?

Another day, another riot
The legion of the faintly praised
Are having problems keeping quiet
I would like their tapes erased.
Here I am in bed at midday
With one of the ones I like
Smoke hangs in the air like music
There are things you can't describe.
I woke up this morning
Two or three or four-four times
I don't like getting up
When it's cold and there's rain outside
You've got love like a new religion
You treat love like a bright crusade
I don't believe in the love religion
I don't drink that lemonade

Another day, another riot
Stuck in fog again
Will I always be this lucky?
Will you always be my friend?

Too much chocolate, number one
Read my story in The Sun
Laugh at all their little lies
Sue till they apologise.
Time and space are playing games with
People who don't understand
You can't talk about the weather
When you've killed the weatherman
How can you continue to
Be human when your job includes
Bugging Freddie Mercury's funeral
Sobbing run as interviews.
And who'll attend your pretty funeral
Persecutor, tabloid scum
Will your best friend disarm the wreaths?
Do you think you'll have a friend to come?
Here I am on stage at midnight
With some of the ones I like
Smoke hangs in the air like music
There are things you can't describe.

I didn't want the night to end,
But now I want the night to end.

Going Public

Minor prophets blushingly approach me
Looking for a sign
Men in charge of corporations flirt with me
I drink their wine
Journalists in eggy suits now
Pester me to tell them lies
Poets I have always hated
Phone me to apologise

I get everything on credit
People make me skip the queue
Hello, I am going public
Who are you?
"Please exploit me," murmur members
Of the pretty girlie class
Pulling off their t-shirts slowly
Baby-oiling tit and ass.

I'm going public
Today while I was buying milk
Girls who wouldn't kiss me once
Stroked me like a piece of silk
All my vices virtues now
My arrogance, my lack of style
Seen in new light, I don't choose how
Glances linger for a while.

"Be a bastard," my world whispers
"Come, we've done the dirty work
Easing down the barriers
Dividing gentleman from jerk
Beat your girl, we'll take a picture
Have some kids, then act their age
In twenty years we'll buy their story
Put it on the People page."

You may raise your hands in horror
When you hear I drink
Give me a degree in higher physics
Every time I think
You may save my breath in bottles
Scrape my spittle from your cheek
Market it as Aristotle's
Sympathetic Magic Treat.

I'm going public.

Don't Scuff My Tan

Don't scuff my tan
I'm a beautiful and angry young man
And who are you
To act the way you do?

(That's how fights begin
Well, the ones I win
The ones fought in my head
Late at night in bed.)

Sirrah, you offend
And so does your friend
I think the time is ripe
To pluck your type

(That's how fights begin
Well, the ones I win
The ones fought in my head
Late at night, in bed.)

Money Loves You

Here inside the city walls
Of Galway, I am taking calls
The hallway's full of other men
Who want to sign me and my friends
I used to worry much too much
About the price of butterscotch
Now I find that I can slouch
Into anybody's mouth
The men who judge these competitions
Ring to offer us positions
Blindfolded and on our backs
With a choice of railway tracks

Money talks, and it says "What would you like?"
Money kisses you and asks "Are you alright?"
Money never denies you its love
Money loves you.

It's the evening before my overnight success
I'm rather tired of this dress
We're renouncing poverty in favour of pelf
It's time to talk about unspeakable wealth
The revolution? The revolution can go fuck.
I had a lucky bullet, but it never brought me luck

Money loves you.

When your mother's music makes more noise
And the astronauts wish they were boys
And the Russians won't play chess these days
And the Times prints 'what-a-mess' clichés
And deeply unattractive men
Are moving through your house again
As the lion tamer's only son
Now rides in on a camel, he
Is sick of lions and has run
Away to join your family...

Money loves you.

Song of the Beggar King

Ah, once I had the world
Now I've even lost my girl
Oh my darling, oh my pearl
How I missed her
But I'm already feeling better
To help me to forget her
I'm going to write a letter
To her sister.

When it happened I was shattered
I really thought it mattered
I was ripped apart and scattered
It was bloody.
Now I stop and smell the flowers
And take too many showers
And prance around for hours
In the nuddy.

I'm losing everything
The cardboard box, the diamond ring
I'm losing everything
So why do I want to dance and sing?

I was handsomer than most
I had a yacht on either coast
I'd got a lot, don't mean to boast
But I owned Armani.
Now I'm living in the gutter
On a half a pound of butter
Get my outfits from the utterly
Salvation Army.

I used to be a pseud
And whistle Mozart in the nude
And think the Rolling Stones were crude

Rude, lewd, and stuff.
Now I spend all day in bed
And sing along to Right Said Fred
And look at pictures of the Med
And it's enough.

I'm losing everything
The Chippendale, the Ming
Losing everything
I am the beggar king.

All this my kingdom.

Tarty Girls

Reckless, wild, uncivilized
Their mothers hate the way they dress
Their fathers going crazy now
Faces painted, hair's a mess
Thigh-high boots and sky-high hair
Flick knives in their underwear, yes
But everybody loves them, man
They couldn't care less

Celebrate the tarty girls
Celebrate the wasted years
When you're with the tarty girls
The whole world disappears
Let's have a party, girls
Let's have the party here
Hear it for the tarty girls
Hear it for us all, my dear

Thigh-high boots and sky-high hair
There's a couple over there
Here's a couple over here
Next year's models, catch them this year
Tarty girls are in effect
Six a.m. the room is wrecked
We fall asleep to MTV
Hurray for tarty girls and me

You can drop the bomb now
We don't care.

Forgotten

Watching late night television
Half in love with Vivien Leigh
But she's so beastly dead now
Isn't she?
And the light that glanced off her's
Enhanced in my direction
By machines that keep her ghost alive
To give me this erection.
Outside, drunken twelve-year olds
Stand laughing at the fire alarms
But oh, that she were young again
And held me in her arms.

The light lags behind you
As you break up and on through
It's dark at the top
But it's dark at the bottom too.
Sometimes it seems
We have dreamt the wrong dreams
As we flare through the arc
From unknown to forgotten.

I know that it's not cool of me
This late in the century
To drop a tear in sympathy
For one dead girl's lost beauty
When I can't cry for bigger things
The girl herself, or all my sins
The holocaust, my coming end
Extinctions, or a vanished friend.
But pretty girls I'll never meet
Can set me stumbling in the street
Ones long dead, like Vivien Leigh
Or ones not born who, when I'm dead
Will feel the same for me.

Big Happy Ending

The Godmothers cometh, out of the attics
Burdened by wisdom and mental rheumatics
Insisting you take their advice and their cake
One as dry as the other, both poisonous as kingsnakes,
The cake Is some Safeways pink plaster disaster
The advice, that you trade in your white Stratocaster
For death.
But every word that you sing
Every note that you're bending
Propels the whole thing towards the big happy ending
You do Top of the Pops, give them money, they take it
And tell their friends down the shops how they helped you to make it.

Certain fathers are sniffing and snorting their usual
Tedious, tiring and tired disapproval
They read your reviews with their red noses wrinkling
Look up, and hiccup, and fake up some twinkling
In those bleary eyes to disguise weary truth
They envy their own children's wonderful youth
They look out the window, annoyed that it's sunny
And say pathetically, "But where's the money?"

But every word that you sing
Every note that you're bending
Propels the whole thing towards the big happy ending
You buy them new places with the fruits of your labours
And they sing your praises to the fucking neighbours.

Galway and Los Angeles

I was in TV reception
Waiting for a taxi
Which I could not afford
When in spun you,
BP, and a camera crew
Through revolving doors
I was pale with lack of recognition
You were sick with fame, and giddy from your high position
Desperate to climb down and take a break
While I stood trembling with the need to make your mistake
And we caught each other's eyes
And our expressions changed
And, with nothing to say, we looked away again

And now in different stages of the same disease
On different continents, we smile and say "please"
And I know that you don't know that I exist
And I can just about live with this
And you know that a million
Speak your name
As radio and TV throw your face and voice around the
    world again
And do we ever sleep at the same time?
Do you think we ever sleep at the same time?
I'm glad that you were beautiful for me when I was nobody
I hope to be as handsome when we catch each other's eyes again

Galway and Los Angeles
Are more than seven hours apart
And in that gap fly aeroplanes
And pretty boys and girls and art
And we cannot communicate
The fans are on the interstate
Tabloid writers tap the lines
That should have been in songs of mine
I'll ring you when my number one

Has turned to random in my hand
And you are not the special one
And Billboard says I understand
Galway and Los Angeles.

BP got me tickets to the show that night
You looked so pretty under television lights
The people that I run into
None of them, no, none of them are you
Some are far too sensible
Very few as beautiful
Very few.
And as my hips rotate between the parted thighs of a girl I like
A flash illuminates her face and, as I hear a motorbike
Roar fast under my window, I see your face, sadly pretty
And an enormous roar of thunder sets off car alarms across the city.
Her hips became your hips.
I came with the wrong name on my lips.

Sometimes I can't sleep
And sometimes I can't wake up

They talk of the drinking
But never the thirst.

Additional lyrics, from 'Galway and Los Angeles (Dragons are Extra version)':

I tend to break into song
You, of course, have your own key
The sales figures say I'm wrong
But I've read your view of the industry.
The ghost of The Go-Betweens stops me from saying you're wrong.

If I bothered you, I didn't mean to,
I had to talk to someone, so I picked on you
Picking on you's the thing to do these days
Everybody's at it.
Everybody's so brave.

An Enormous Request

Sometimes you skip like a girl
And sometimes you skip like a stone
And the stage is a playground build to your design
And you dance on like you're all alone
But you're not alone
In a hall full of people that you don't know
And don't want to, Christ
Look at them go,
Dragging their drunk friends
Down to the front end
And you turn to go

But the boyfans roar
Their enormous request
And a thousand little girls
Want to wear your dress
And your name is so loud in your ears
You can't hear any more
For the boyfans' roar

And the statue you became
Beneath the floodlights, will remain
Their only memory of you.
In the studio dark you can turn into
Tarka the Otter if you want
You can fall down like Bozo the Clown
You can stand on your hands
You can eat with your feet holding chopsticks
Or drop-kick a tape into Studio Two,
Be a woman or a girl, sing the sensual world
or watch Scooby-Doo, chainsmoke Gauloise Blue
When E.M.I. call, put a cushion on the phone...
Live a life with a family, books, friends and privacy
It's just like reality, a life of your own

And all you recall of that stage you went through
When you were nineteen, and the world looked at you
Are the remnants of dreams that you can't believe true.

Thanks For The Clothes

A great face
Beestung soul
Thanks for the clothes.
I wish I loved you
Like I love your city
I wish I loved you
God, you're pretty
A New York girl with mid-west eyes
A poetry
Of breast and thigh
As I lie above you
How I'd love to love you.
You lie on the roof like a statue of silver
Under a New York moon
Just one of ten million lights
Left burning tonight.
This party will be over soon.

No sixties for you
You're one of the few
People I know
Who live in their own time.

And if my plane
Should roll down the runway
in a ball of flame
My last wish
Would be to
Have loved you.
Thanks for the clothes
Thanks for the meals
Thanks for not making a scene
In the court of appeals.

Looking at young women
Pleased that they exist
I call them girls
They forgive me for this
I forgive them
For not being mine
Everyone's having
A wonderful time

What I think I need tonight
Is the wrong girl
Not the right.

Thanks for the pizzas
Thanks for the beans
The Paris, France T-shirt
And Japanese jeans
Thanks for the clothes
Thanks for the meals
Thanks for not making a scene
In the court of appeals.

All my favourite poets
In love with their best lovers
Write about the others
So obliquely.

Heretic Boulevard

When our revolution comes
The gutters will run with champagne
When our revolution comes
The streets will be painted
In violent colours
And given new names
And given new names...

When our revolution comes
We shall stride down
Heretic Boulevard...

And if we should die
Before that great day
Well, at least we tried
And we would have died anyway.

(*Another Day, Another Riot* originally ended with
a new recording of Galway Bay.)

Mindless Optimism

(Toasted Heretic, 1994)

(*Mindless Optimism* also contained a new recording of 'Here Comes
The New Year'.)

Maybe We Should Talk

Waiting for my test to come through
Me and her
A mouthful of rockets and you
You were there too
Waiting
Waiting for my test to come through.

I'm kneeling at the fountain
I've come down from the mountain
Kid, the revolution was a bust.
All the stuff I wanted
It turned out I didn't want it
I threw away the money for her trust.

A broken heart
A broken bone
A bed of rock
A bed of stone.

She is loyal.

Maybe we should talk
Maybe we…

You left all your flags on the moon
Didn't you?

You told me that you'd be home soon
That wasn't true
Left me
Patient
Waiting for my test to come through.
I'm learning
To love winter
Now that winter's all I've got.
It really is so beautiful
I don't know how to get across.

There's something going on that I can't spell
I got hard in New York, can't you tell?
Your life is such a drama, but the books don't sell
Why don't you shoot yourself?

Maybe we…
Maybe we should talk.

Passenger Jets

"Throw me a beat and a line
And I'll be fine
If you throw me a beat and a line."
Can you say that for true?
Can you say that for real?
If I said that to you
Would you laugh at the deal
If I threw you a beat and a line?
So I throw you Kerouac, I throw you cocaine
And you throw it back and I throw it back at you again
Throw you a beat and a line.

Passenger jets of the depressed
Crash into hills, crash into hills
Of train wrecks, bad sex and sleeping pills

Evinrude, yeah
Collect me later.

I'm chewing rocks to sand
I want "I Wanna Hold Your Hand"
My death is in demand
This plane's about to land.
At passport control they say
"What do you do
And to who do you belong?
Do you belong?"
And I say I belong to a girl
And I write love songs.

Lightning

We sheltered in the ruins from the shower
The rain poured through the vanished roof for half an hour
Dry by a wall, we look up at the sky
Lightning comes, scribbles on my eye
You laugh, we kiss, dazzled by its power
And thunder comes, and lightning blasts the tower
Oh, don't be afraid, it's only lightning
Don't be afraid, it's only lightning

This is not a firedrill
This is not an exercise
This is not some kind of simulation, kid, with extra lives
But don't be afraid. It's only lightning
And we're young
We're young enough
I'll be alright
If you'll be tough
Here we stand
Lightning-struck
In wonderland
Oh, wish me luck

The lightning never struck
We didn't really kiss
We had a lot of luck
But not in this.
Love, well I was never into love
Like, I had a lot of time for like
Lightning's just a metaphor that I am none the better for
It was love of course that didn't strike
In the same place, twice
And like, well, like is very nice.
Oh don't be afraid, it's only lightning
And like, of course, is very nice.

Anglepoise Park

Marry me? No. You can't even stay awake.
Come back when you're twenty
And your hands don't shake.
I'll pass the time writing anthems for countries that do not exist
But I don't think you
Can get a tattoo
To cover the places I kissed
There you are, with your dreams that make sense
There you are
With your dreams
That make sense

Praying for the dark in Anglepoise Park
A is for amphetamine
Praying for the dark in Anglepoise Park
B is for boyfriend
Praying for the dark in Anglepoise Park
See you sometime
You're praying for the dark in Anglepoise Park
Do come again

But he won't shut down
And he won't shut up.

Golden year, golden year, J.F.K., the fear of fear
You looked up to tell me, this is neat
And blew
My mind
All over the back seat.

Walking home through a popcorn blizzard
Is this snow?
Is this snow?
When winter hit the summerhouse
Well, it had to go.

Did she tie them up with ribbon?
Did she dump them in the river?
Did she know what she was doing
And assume that I'd forgive her?

Praying for the dark in Anglepoise Park
A is for amphetamine
Praying for the dark in Anglepoise Park
B is for boyfriend
Praying for the dark in Anglepoise Park
See you sometime
You're praying for the dark in Anglepoise Park
Do come again

It's All Over

We were lonely and confused
The past had faded out before the town was out of view
I checked the mirror, but I couldn't look at you
And they're upset
The deals you cut, the mess you left
I know you'll say they asked for it
But really there's no need for it
I really wish to God you'd quit
While you're this far ahead
You've got her in your bed
You've broken all her other lovers' backs
The time has come
The time has come and gone and come again to just relax.

You've won
Home free
You've come
One two and three
It's all over.
Leave the wounded to recover.

Please don't take this wrong
Please don't ask me what I'm on
I've been your friend for far too long
To have to talk to you in song.
I'm sick of hearing troop reports
When all I've asked is how you are
You've taken this war far too far
Far too far.
Have mercy on your few surviving friends
I'm saying this in friendship, not in self-defence
Have mercy on your few surviving friends
I'm saying this because I used to like you, not in self-defence.
It's all over.

Heart Attack

You can stay here, if you like
I've changed my mind about my life
When you ran your ship onto my rock
I couldn't believe it, I'm still in shock.
Things go wrong, it's still O.K.
You know that you don't have to stay
The future happens anyway
Have you ever tried to stop it?

They cut the tree, the tree grows back
The guy recovers from the heart attack
It's two steps forward, only one step back
We're all going to get there some day.
Some day.

The terraces of love, the courtship wall
The spires above the kissing mall
The chandeliers in love's great hall
Plunge as beams decay and fall.
It was just a building after all
Just a building after all.
The chandeliers in love's great hall
Plunge as beams decay and fall.

Mummy, Are We There Yet?

When I was young, the world my toy
I was such a clever boy
I could describe the way I felt
In ways that made the pretty melt

Was I wrong?
Was I bad?
Was I bold?
Will this song
Make us sad
When we're old?

Oh, mummy, are we there yet? Daddy, are we there yet?
Mummy, are we there yet?

And though they ran the trains
Of cattle trucks and live remains
Around the towns in the early days
Late at night, on the freight railways
You could hear the sobbing miles away
"Mummy, are we there yet?"

Living In My Time

In a century a dog might choke
On the bones of your beautiful face
And I won't be there to care
I won't be there to care

I want to be simple
I want to be good
Don't want to be lonely
I'd love you if I could

But I'm living in my time.

And the moon grows dark
And the room grows dark
And clouds park right above the flat
And I don't think I'm asleep yet
And I wish I didn't cry like that

It's O.K. if you don't make sense
Don't try so hard, and trust your friends
Trip the safeties
Risk the bends
More to follow

Message ends.

Don't Tell Me We Don't Live

The nights I should have stayed at home,
I didn't stay at home
The past that you forgive
Days I spent the rent,
Still had to pay the rent
Oh baby, don't tell me we don't live.

I look like a nightclub in daylight tonight
But I feel like a million of something bright
Do you get déjà vu with that déjà vu?
Well, maybe you don't, but I do.
Oh baby, don't tell me we don't live.

Don't tell me we don't live.

B-sides, unreleased tracks, and post-Toasted Heretic lyrics:

Food For Breakfast

Well, it's back to food for breakfast now you've gone.
It was good of you to stick around so long.
So long to your winning morning ways,
As tongue and lip and nipple tip would graze
The bits of me that woke up before I did
The way you'd toss a coin when undecided
Which pair of perfect lips you'd wake me up with…

Call around sometime, and share a cup with me.

Neither mental nor stability were ever either of your middle names.
Your wonderful ability to improvise at early morning games
Was a constant source of joy to me,
In particular I now recall
Your game of throw the Christmas tree into the street
Then slowly bang the headboard through the wall

But it's back to food for breakfast now you've gone
Oh it's back to food for breakfast now you've gone

I can swiftly walk right through the door now,
I can slowly walk wrong through the window.
I'm pretty much as free as anybody can be
Thank you for giving this pleasure to me
But the best of your presents I think you'll agree
Involved lipstick at dawn, and were half an hour long
As the baby-oiled shaft penetrated you laughed and said
"So, when I go, will you turn me to song?"

And of course I did, God you were better than buttered
Hot crumpet with strong black coffee at dawn

But it's back to food for breakfast now you've gone
Oh it's back to food for breakfast now you've gone
It was good of you to stick around so long.

So long.

(B-side of 'Another Day, Another Riot'.)

Ha Ha Ha

I'm going to tell the truth tonight, tonight's a night for telling truth
I have got a little Ruth, you couldn't call me ruthless
But in a time when teeth are potent
Neither could you call me
Toothless
To strain a rhyme a little, as little as I can
It's hard to tell the truth and make it scan.

Oh all I'm going to end up saying is, I think I'm perfect
Goodbye to a decade of check out my haircut
Here are the nineties, the nineties are mine,
You can forget this song in nineteen ninety nine.
Dated, I've been dated, and it's felt fine
The rest of the century is mine.

And hey hey hey, a happy band of friends
Are burning down the offices of older men
And ha ha ha, be my friend, the magazines have lost the trend
Again.
And again and again and again.

"I can't get up!"
"We're sending help immediately, Mrs. Fletcher."
"See? Protect yourself with Lifecall and you're never alone."

My friends had a party, it made the national press
'Cause they've so little fun, that we've got all that's left
The headlines say sporadic bursts of youthful laughter in the west.

(Extra track on the 12" of 'Another Day, Another Riot'.)

137

Meet Mr. Morrison

Here comes Mr Morrison, as happy as my hat,
Everybody loves you when you're bald and fat.
Here comes Mr Morrison, cheers and down the hatch,
Everybody loves you when you scowl and scratch.
Here comes Mr Morrison, let's put up a plaque,
Everybody loves you when you wish you were black.

Here comes Mr Morrison, back from Billy Bunter's,
Everybody loves you when you won't talk to the punters.
Here comes Mr Morrison, as jolly as the Berlin Wall,
Everybody loves you when you fire your crew for bugger all.
Here comes Mr Morrison, applause destroys the city,
Everybody loves you when you're crippled with self-pity.

Oh ho ho, oh ho ho ho uh huh,
I remember when Curly Wurlys were three pee
Three pee three pee, and twice as long, twice as long
Stuffin' my face with cake, uh, stuffin' my face with cake
Potted shrimp, with a limp
Boogaloogaloogaloo,
Rave on, rave on, rave on
Rave on Dr Who
Rave on Bill and Ben,
The flower pot men,
Rave on...

(Extra track on the 12" of 'Another Day, Another Riot'.)

Living at the Wrong Speed

I wake up and hear a voice
Say "I'm lonely."
It's my voice.
Miserable
As a little kid
I kicked you out
I'm glad I did.

The earth sucks
At the soles of our shoes
Sucks at the souls of our friends
Gravity hates us
For dancing again
So soon after dancing again.

In neither each other nor God do we trust
I wish I could do all the things that I must
I wish that I had all the things that I need
But I'm living at the wrong speed.

(B-side of 'Galway and Los Angeles'.)

It Makes the Sex Exciting
When There's Been a Bit of Fighting

1

The stone wants to be a stone
You want to be alone.

Well I'm screwing all the girls
That I didn't screw
While I was going out with you.

It makes the sex exciting
When there's been a bit of fighting

2

When does life begin?
At birth, or on a whim.
Can I begin mine then?
Of course you fucking can.

My teens didn't work
 So I got my money back

I drove a pedal-car of angst
When all my friends were driving tanks

3

It makes the sex exciting
When there's been a bit of fighting

And there's always the cunts
Who hang around your girlfriend for months

It makes the sex exciting
When there's been a bit of fighting

4

I spent a cold night on Media Mountain

Raised by hyenas
On sour milk
And complimentary peanuts
Small town boy makes good

Will he be broken by
The rising cost of getting high
Will he be broken by
The rising cost of getting high?

Small town boy makes good

5

You can lead the rising star
To the complimentary bar
But you can't make him drink
Small town boy makes good

How thin would you like your fame sliced sir?
How thin would you like your fame sliced sir?

You drag the star
From the wreckage of his car
But you can't stop him drinking
It's a public fountain
A night on Media Mountain
Ten seconds and counting

6

I'd rather get
Laid in the shade
Than stand
Sneering in a clearing.
How wearing.

7

I don't want a quote
In your suicide note
But as you used to say
Before blowing me away
It makes the sex exciting
When there's been a bit of fighting

8

The fog comes in off the sea
But it's OK
The blind boy never gets to see
But it's OK
The drug trial doesn't save the child
But it's OK
The stray dog dies in the wild
But it's OK
The peacekeeper steps on a mine
But it's OK
She won't get the letter in time
But it's OK

9

I gave you my love and so forth all that stuff for what it was
worth and it wasn't enough

10

It makes the sex exciting
When there's been a bit of fighting

We've proved we're doing it for love
Now give us the money.

(Recorded with Melanie Houston, under the name Buggercult)

Satellite Dishes

With legs that long
You'd think she'd fall over
And, oh, you'd be right
I tried to be good last night
I wasn't bad

Mess up your life, it's great
I've messed up mine
And I feel so much better
So much of the time
It won't make much difference
This late in the game
We all know
Much too much
To complain

Pretending we know
Less than we do
Just to get through
It won't make much difference
This late in the game
We all know
Much too much
To complain

I came to these islands
On a boat that carried
Satellite dishes
And beautiful girls

I came to these islands
On a boat that carried
Satellite dishes
And beautiful girls

The star that you wished on last year
Has been taken down for repair
So you sit on your own
In a room full of white noise
And dead air.

Adventures of Ulysses

The huge and one-eyed bouncer roars, enraged
As I glide by him, hanging from your fleece
We're pouring out like smoke from the dancing cave
Onto the great black river of the street

Living this enormous life
This early night, this summer heat
Living this enormous life
Licking honey from your feet

Is there one who understands me?
Is there one who'll lend me a fiver?
Is there one who'll get some cans for me
And we'll go down to the river

Honey I'm a survivor
Ship-wrecked, prick-teased
Head hurts when I sneeze
Job lost, car seized,
No way home, on my knees
I won't break
Call me Ulysses

Living this enormous life
Every one of us an equal
Living this enormous life
There will never be a sequel

And we get some cider and go down to the beach
And I can hear the sirens in the car-park singing each to each
And the music of the sirens going in and out of phase
Is as beautiful as violence to your enemy's face

Of arms and the man I sing
Of legs and the woman too
Of sex and the single girl
Of kids with nothing to do

Living this enormous life
Whether they want to or not
Living this enormous life
On the estate that time forgot.

The warriors of clubland lean on their spears
They say, Ulysses, tell us what we wish to hear
I say I've seen all things in heaven above
And the greatest of these is love, boys
The greatest of these is love

Loving this enormous life
Whether we want to or not
Loving this enormous life
On the world that God forgot.

On the world that God forgot.

Living this enormous life.
Every one of us an equal.
Living this enormous life.

There will never

Be a sequel.

(Set to David Holmes' 'Don't Die Just Yet', & recorded as by
The PiggyBackGang)

Pregnant

We eat what we kill
We fall in love and we get each other pregnant
We didn't get it together today but we will
We always come to some arrangement

We eat what we kill
We fall in love and we get each other pregnant
We didn't get it together today but we will
We always come to some arrangement

We just eat the lotus
Gentlemen, with the odd thug
Don't quote us
If you're talking to the drug squad

It's springtide and the wind is up
The river backs into the lake
The Corrib takes your paper cup
Like gravity was some mistake
Flows backwards under bridges
From the ocean to the lake
Flows backwards under bridges
Brings the suicides to life
Gives bicycles and fridges back
To little kids and someone's wife
It's spring tide and the wind is pushing
Water backwards up the river
Somehow it is still surprising
Even children point, and shiver

At a sign that doesn't mean a thing
The suicides will not come back to life
And she won't find her wedding ring
In the fish her husband caught tonight

But we eat what we kill
We fall in love and we get each other pregnant
We didn't get it together today but we will
We'll come to some arrangement

We mean what we say
And it always turns out OK
Doesn't it?

We just eat the lotus
Gentle men, with the odd thug
Don't quote us
If you're talking to the drug squad

Stay home tonight,
Wrap up warm and sit tight
This weather just means weather
It's a storm

A storm in a small bay
It'll strip off some slates
While we play poker through the powercut
With our mates

But we eat what we kill
We fall in love and we get each other pregnant
Didn't get it together tonight but we will
We always come to some arrangement

We mean what we say
And it always turns out OK
Doesn't it?

(Set to Leftfield's 'Melt', & recorded as by *The PiggyBackGang*)

About the author

Julian Gough was born in London, to
Tipperary parents. When he was seven, the
family returned to Tipperary. He was
educated by the Christian Brothers, back
when throwing a boy across the room was
considered healthful exercise for both
parties. At university in Galway, he began
writing and singing with the underground
literary rock band Toasted Heretic. They
released four albums, and had a top ten hit in
Ireland in 1991 with 'Galway and Los Angeles', a song about not
kissing Sinéad O'Connor.

Photo: Anne Marie Fives

His first novel, *Juno & Juliet*, was published in 2001. His
second, *Jude: Level 1*, came six years later. *Jude: Level 1* was
described by the Sunday Tribune as "possibly the finest comic
novel since Flann O'Brien's *The Third Policeman*". In the UK, it
was shortlisted for the Everyman Wodehouse Prize for Comic
Fiction. Will Self, controversially, won. Gough – understandably
miffed – kidnapped Will Self's pig, and posted the ransom video
on Youtube.

In 2007, his story 'The Orphan and the Mob' won the BBC
National Short Story Prize – then the world's largest annual prize
for a single short story.

He also wrote the first short story ever printed in the Financial
Times, 'The Great Hargeisa Goat Bubble'. In 2009, 'The Great
Hargeisa Goat Bubble' was broadcast as an acclaimed radio play
on BBC Radio 4.

In early 2010, the Sunday Tribune chose *Jude: Level 1* as their
Irish Novel of the Decade.

His third novel, *Jude in London*, will be published by Old Street
in September 2010.